Poems

from the heart

Prayers

from the soul

Poems from the Heart, Prayers from the Soul

The moral right of the author has been asserted.

This is a work of fiction.

Any references to historical events, real people, or real places are used fictitiously. Other names, characters, places, and events are products of the author's imagination, and any resemblance to actual events or places or persons, living or dead, is entirely coincidental.

Cover design © Creative Covers Design
Formatting and editing by Rebecca Weeks

Poems from the Heart, Prayers from the Soul.

I am me

There are a few versions of me, some I like and some I can't bear, there is also that one special version that is truly not of this world, he views this world through the eyes of the divine, feeling humbled to know such beautiful souls. Then there is the horrid frightened me who has been so hurt by his journey to this point, sometimes he is even too scared to say a simple hello in case another harsh lesson is thrust upon him. They are all me, I cannot change them sometimes I wish I could.

God, I hurt

Why can no one understand the pain I carry.
Was I so bad to be punished this way?
An angel who walks the earth to carry the
misery of man.
Lord forgive me for I carry the burden of
sin.
I was kissed upon the brow by the holiest.
As the devil screamed at another soul, that
enters paradise.

Love

Two Angels stood behind a little boy as he says his prays before bed. Such innocence and love were spoken within the words he said Lord, I want to thank you for all the things I have. My sister, my cat and granny and don't forget mum and dad. I loved all my presents, new toys so I can play... Especially Eric my spider who keeps my sister away Lord please help my granny. I think she is very sick My mummy was crying when they came back from their trip They had been to see the doctors, to make her well again He gave her lots of medicine, to take away her pain. I do love all my toys, but special granny's best. She always gives me sweets and makes me wear a vest. So, if lord you can help her, my toys are yours to keep I`ll be good for like forever, and always go to sleep so I'll say goodnight now lord, it's time to go to bed I hope you listened carefully to all the things I said.

Amen

. ° ° . . ° ° .
°   °

Wings of Love

Take my hand little one. Have no fear.
I've watched you from the moment of birth,
from your first whisper in this world till
your last tear.
Yet here I stand in the shadow of your soul.
I feel the love you send into the world and I
feel your pain. know you are never alone
even in your darkest hour I'll stand by your
side. I am love, I am light, all things in this
world are ordained by the most high.
Do not faultier, even though doubt and fear
fills your being. Love of another can
illuminate our souls. To journey on in search
of the truth of self is the destiny of man. To
take the first step of an unknown journey is
fearful, yet I will walk with you.
I will hold your hand when you fear the
darkness. Wipe your tears when you feel all
hope is lost. Have courage little one for I
will never leave you for I am love.

When

When you hide from the world. Well, here
I'll stand.
When you push me away. Well, here I'll
stand.
When you ask your feelings. Well, here I'll
stand.
When life gets scary. Well, here I'll stand.
When you 're filled with doubt. Well, here
I'll stand.
When you look for answers. Well, here I'll
stand.
When you need that shoulder to cry on.
Well, here I'll stand.
When you don't understand life's path.
Well, here I'll stand.
When you need to smile. Well, here I'll
stand.
When you 're finally ready. Well, here I'll
stand.
I'll stand and wait for the silent soul who
welcomes the dawn of a new day
Who's soul sings the praises of the most
high?
Just so you know. WELL, HERE I STAND.

Who?

Who are you?
Who are you to touch my soul?
Who are you to keep me from sleep?
Who are you that knows me so well?
Who are you that walks my path?
Who are you that awakens the sun?
Who are you that kisses the moon?
Who are you that dances in the rain?
Who are you that stole my heart?
Who are you that has given me hope?
Who are you that has given me peace?

Was it too much to ask?

To be honest with each other.
To be there for each other.
To have faith in what we have built.
To grow closer instead of apart.
To forgive and forget.
To accept us at our worst.
To love us at our best.
To say sorry when we are in the wrong.
To remember the past as it happened.
To accept each other's faults.
To cherish our life and love.
To remember there is two in our
relationship.
To not run to another at the first sign of
difficulty.

I guess it was.

The Rhythm of One

Step into the silence.
Look into your dreams.
Join the sacred circle.
Where man and God convene.

The sweet song of the universe.
Is played for you alone.
So cast away your sorrows.
And stand beneath the throne.

She calls to all who listen.
Who has stood apart too long?
It's time to leave the shadows.
Come listen to her song.

She sings a hymn of learning.
Of love and life reborn.
She speaks of ancient teachings.
And knowledge now forswore.

The universe is calling.

The dance of life goes on.
It brings a change of season.
For love to build upon.
As you listen to the heartbeat.
It echoes through your soul.
The future stands before you.
With peace your final goal.

Fae

Do you believe in fairies so small and slim
and sleek? Who hides beneath the moonlight
and play while you 're asleep? They're
mother nature's little helpers, to see them is
so rare. Go seek beneath the bushes and you
might find them there.

Lady of the Cave

I have an amazing friend across the sea.
She lives in truth and purity.
Yet she is scared to unleash her heart.
Her life's been broken from the start.
She hides in a cave not in or out.
Her love of life so much in doubt.
I gave her my heart as a light to see.
And prayed she would come walk with me.
We got to the entrance the light so bright.
But with tear filled eyes she then took flight.
My flame went out .then darkness fell.
Now in that cave, my heart does dwell.
So my hand now stretches across land and
sea.
In the hope, she will finally walk with me.

Child of the Goddess

I see you search for beauty. I see you yearn
for peace. So, come with me, my sister. your
fears shall find release. you sit alone in the
darkness. Within the God's gaze. Come
walk the path of wisdom. I'll guide you
through its maze. Can you hear the ticking?
That clock of father time? Can you feel the
beauty? The love of the divine? your heart is
filled with love. A gift that I have seen.
Come step into the fire. Where man and god
convene. you search across the shadows. As
laughter fills your ears. As candles burn so
brightly. To banish all your fears. your eyes
rest on the saucer. you set to feed the cat.
It's so empty and forgotten. As she takes her
nap. your eyes behold the wonder. The lady
stands so bright. Her fae now moves in
chorus. To a dance of love and light. They
bestow a gift of greeting. From an age now
long ago. A fairy kiss to grace your lips.
And warm your very soul. To give thanks
for all the love you send. In this saddened

world of men. To show you 're not forgotten. My dear beloved friend.

Whispers

The Greatest light looked upon the realm of
man Sensing great loss and confusion as his
children walked their path Saddened by this
he called forth his angels Hence he issued
this command. From this time forth, each
soul on earth Shall be guided by the
heavenly host When asked how, they could
serve this wish The lord Replied, you shall
be the breath on their lips. The compassion
in their hearts, their reason to forgive. their
light in the darkness When all is lost and
they call to the heavens you shall stand by
their side bringing comfort and love you will
spread my love and wisdom as you guide
their journey through life Mankind's
language will be that of love and forgiveness
When they sleep you shall whisper the truth
of creation and these truths they shall speak
as if they were their very own words. From
that time forth mankind's shadow hid the
host of heaven Always there but not always
seen.

Where did you go?

I turned for second and you were gone. I stood beside you through thick and thin. We laughed together, we cried together you were my light in the darkness. I felt your sadness. I am sorry I could do no more. I fell asleep. No pain just love and light. As the year turns for one moment I feel you and hear your voice. you bring gifts yet cannot hear me. I touch your red tear stained face as you look on. I love you but where did you go. I sat and watched through all these years. With a broken heart and endless tears I want you to love, to laugh, to live This would be my greatest gift to give We can never be that far apart For you will always rest within my heart.

Rip Louise

So, loved and so missed.

One

One kiss to last a thousand years. your soul
is joined with mine. I`ll wrap you in my
loving arms until the end of time. I have
only ever seen your face. I never heard your
name. My heart and soul are yours to keep.
As we dance within our flame.

Noddy

I have a friend named Noddy, she sleeps one hour a night. To see her in the morning is such a scary sight. she loves to sing and dance, but Madonna she is not.

But if you dare to tell her, the language gets quite hot.

She has a cat named Simon, a vicious scary mite.

If you try to stroke him, you 'll probably get a bite. I fell for that trick last time, all cute and cuddly was he, but the look on his face, made me want to flee so next time I shall visit, body armour I will wear or maybe just to be safe I'll stand on a chair

Would you believe me?

If I told you. Two hearts can beat as one. If I told you. Two souls sing the same song of love. If I told you. Two people can lead the same life. If I told you. Two people share the same thoughts. If I told you. Two people shared the same pain. If I told you. Two people can speak to each other without saying a word. If I told you. Two people have shared the same loss. If I told you. Two people can act as one. If I told you. Two people cry the same tears at the same time. If I told you. Two people were joined by god. If I told you. Two people lost their marbles at the same time. If I told you. Two people walked through the same shadows at the same time, unaware the other was near.

If I told you. Two people have been at death's door at the same time but too many miles apart If I told you. Two people feel so lost that life has no meaning without the other. Well, I have felt this and this is truth.

Oh, Shadows of the World

Have you ever looked at the pain you bring?
Did you hear the song of sorrow the angels
sing? Did you see the tears fall and hearts
broken? Did you listen to so many prayers
spoken?
The blood you spilt in no Gods name. What
was the point what did you gain? Broken
lives and tortured souls. Carnage and
mayhem your only goal.
Now angels weep as man cries out. Lost in
darkness, so full of doubt. you 're just the
shadows, no light you hold. Just Full of hate,
as you spread the lies you 're told.
the Gods light still burns the flame of love.
As they watch over us from above. As
mankind strives once more for peace. So, all
their pain can find release.

Coffee

Every day when I wake up, my first thought
is the coffee cup. I rush from bed, to shower,
then dress. Then try and fight through the
bedroom's mess. To find my shoes and
brush my hair then the earrings, oh that
special pair. Downstairs is next, past the
kids and him. To find out the kettle was not
plugged in. I search the cupboards for that
jar of bliss. Stopping to grab my morning
kiss. Hubby moans that breakfasts comes
first. there is not a chance I need to quench
my thirst. The kettles boiled now the cup is
full. This has become my favourite brew.

The King's Savior

The wind howled as the fallen king fought
his way through the dark forest. His castle
burned only ashes remain. His wife and only
child had entered deaths domain.
The rain fell like tears from Heaven. All was
lost. Nothing remained just a broken heart
and a life of pain. A clearing ahead not far
now. a chance to rest to catch his breath. To
sit and rest and remember all those lives he
left.
He struggled on each footstep to walk a
mighty task. Each gasping breath he took
felt like it was his last. He fell to his knees
beneath a tall wild oak. Unable to go on. His
life slipped into a darkened place where the
sun never shone.
How many days or nights he slept is truly
not known. His first glimpse of the world
was the sun resting on its heavenly throne.
His body ached just pain and grief no limb
was left not sore. He struggled to rise but
once again he fell to the forest floor.

His eyes opened gazing upon a flower so
rare and pure. Tears filled his eyes as its
beauty filled his core. Filled with the wonder
of the scene before his eyes. its divine scent
carried by the breeze to fill the sunlit skies.
As days and weeks went by he tried but
found he could not leave. He just sat and
watched this wondrous gift of divine
reprieve. All his past was lost filled with
sorrow and such pain. But nothing but this
time and place did only remain.
I shall call you Linda for a beauty you surely
are. you light up the forest like the evening's
brightest star. Winter did arrive and his new
found love now slept. He just lay beneath
the oak ensuring her safety kept.
Time went by and the seasons always
change. yet he still did not leave through
sun, wind, or rain.
As winter came and Linda slept the
king stood guard once more. His entire
kingdom had now become the wild forest
floor
As each day passed the king grew tired a
young man he was not his cloak wrapped
tight as he hugged his small fire at peace
with his lot He struggled to stay on this

earthly realm death called, but stay he must
just to glimpse her beauty once more. Before
he returned to dust
winter faded day by day. But, the king was
very weak He cried unto the heavens for the
spring that he did seek. So down beside his
love, the king did finally lay. praying to the
gods above for just another day
The night did pass and Linda awoke to the
call of the rising sun and to sadly find her
guardians time had finally come through the
forest travellers came upon this sacred place.
To find the late king with a look of peace
upon his face
resting upon the trusty oak all pain and grief
had gone guarding his beloved as the forest
sang its song.

. ° °   .   .   ° °
°   ■   ■   ■   °

The Watchers

The figures we cast in wood and stone. To place on a shelf left all alone. Some are lovers yet some are fae. They sit and watch us throughout the day

We're so busy in this world of ours. From Hot summer days to April showers. We move them, once or twice a week. Just to find the dust we seek.

A trusty hound who has now long passed cast in china so his memory lasts a little boy or girl or lady and gent filled with a love that's heaven sent

They all live somewhere within your home. All apart from the garden gnome. He sits in your garden to tend and care along with the fairies you might find there.

Tara

I stood upon the Hill of Tara its beauty was so vast the centuries disappeared, I was lost in a time now past. So many had stood here, from kings to the humble man they walk upon the stony path to gaze upon this land I have gifted the tree of healing for those we know in pain. A simple little token to help their health regain I have touched the _Lia Fáil_ the seat of many kings. who touched this sacred stone so the world could hear it sing.

Angels

Angels, angels they are everywhere. they
kissed your soul to show they care. They
stood by you through tears and joy. They
held your hand to welcome your baby boy

They listen to all your fears and woes. And
even when you stub your toes. They never
moan or close their ears. There always there
to wipe your tears.

So please doubt them not, and just sit and
wait. For that posh frock you want or that
new garden gate. For them to send healing
to your ailing Gran. They were sent by god
to help when they can.

Hands

One finger for the smile on your face. One finger to kiss your lips. One finger to hear your laughter. One finger to wipe your tears. One finger to calm your fears. One finger to watch you sleep One finger to care when you are sick. One finger to hand you my heart. The right thumb to show that I will always be there. The left thumb to show that I will always care. Now I close my hands so they never part. To closely guard your precious Heart

My Wish for you

That no tear shall ever mark your face. That
your heart is filled with grace. That when
the darkest clouds unfurl That your smile
shall light up the world

That you shall never feel alone. That no pain
shall find its home. That you find peace in
every way That no worries shall fill your
day

That you sleep so sound and true. That no
one ever can make you blue. That you sing
and laugh and dance. That you give life one
more chance

That whatever you eat you will never feel
fat. That you are loved just like your cat
That your journey far and never tire. That
your soul will never lose its fire.

My wish for you is peace and love. With the
odd Blessing from above.

The Song of truth

Raise your voice and sing your song. stand
up proud and sing it loud. Wipe your eyes
and dry your tears. It is time to tell the world
your fears.

They said that you couldn't, that you were
no good. They were not worthy of the
ground you stood. They laughed as you fell
and now cry as you rise. you were just a
figure they came to despise.

It was never you, it was always them. they
cannot taint this hidden gem. your light shall
blaze among the stars. so that so many
others may journey far.

So, stand tall once more, and sing your song.
To show the world that you belong.

Can you?

Can you feel the rain as it falls on your face?
Can you feel the memories we built in this
place? Can you hear the echoes as children
laugh and play? Can you hear the words
your heart cries out to say?

Can you hear the songs, that we made our
very own? Can you see the house that we
made into our home? Can you hear my voice
as it speaks from way above? Can you hear
our vows so true and full of love?

Can you hear the tears, I cried when you had
gone? Can you feel me there, as you listen to
our song? Can you find the strength to live
again once more? Can you see my footprints
as you walk along the shore?

Our love will last forever, I'll wait each day
for you? I'll stand within your shadow, as I
gently watch over you?

When I looked upon
the mirror

I saw you. A reflection of the best parts of
me I thought of your beauty and felt love. I
thought of your tears and felt a sadness lost
in time. I thought of your laughter and my
heart sang. I thought of your smile and the
beauty of the heavens faded. I thought of
your heart and was lost in the presence of
such beauty. I thought of your soul and the
angels bowed down to worship you I
thought of your eyes and found myself lost.
I thought of your lips and felt unworthy to
kiss them.
I thought of you and at last found me.

. ॱ ॰ ॰ ॱ . ॱ ॰ ॰ ॱ . ॰

Tears of heaven

So, they placed me on a hill and nailed me
to a cross.

To gaze upon this world to feel its pain and
loss I called upon my father, to forgive their
errant ways. To stand and watch over them
until their end of days

The tears fell down from Heaven as angels
wept in vain.

To stand and watch their father's only son
suffer so much pain Thunder filled the skies
as the might of the heavens roared.

To watch his gift to this world just nailed
upon a board

So many stood and watched me with my
cross to bear But Only a blessed few chose
my love to share.

The twelve stations I have taken each step
for the heart of man There was No deceit or
sorrow found upon my plan

I came to bring a message of love and life
reborn. To guide the soul of man is the vow
that I have sworn Now I leave to join my
father as he sits upon his throne. For those
who choose to follow me, Heaven will be
your home.

. ° °   .   . ° °   .
° ■   ■   ■   °

From the chaos of the universe

From the chaos of the universe, I emerged
plunged into this nightmare called life. I
seek only peace and love. yet the world
taunts my every attempt. I walk buried deep
within my own truth. People come and
people go but this life last cannot last
forever and once more I am cast back into
the void of divine consciousness.
I sat on this hilltop and look out onto the
world. All I saw was trees and grass, no sign
of man. I could hear the birds singing and
the bees working their magic on the flowers
of the earth. I wondered what this world
would be like without man to show his hand.
how much would change, would it be better
or worse. Well, the rain would still fall and
the sun would still rise. the seasons would
still turn. mother nature would still care for
all in her kingdom. Birth and death would
still come and when needed. you could

honestly feel the world was better before man arrived. Man brought pain to the earth in the name of progress. apart from the elements how could the world fight back? They tore down the forests, they hunted to extinction, nothing in the animal kingdom was safe. they brought poisons to fill the air and sea. Taking without question what they thought was their birthright. Did they ever think of the effect they had? Not that I can recall. you would think man would realise that everything comes with a price. Yet they continue their path of evolution. I wonder how much will be left when they are done. How many of my kin will be forgotten? How many of my cubs will never get the chance to run in the fields? How much longer will they set the hounds on us in the name of sport? We can but hope that man will evolve then leave the world they ravaged in the hands of its true owners.

Sometimes we all have to take a step back and remember why we chose to walk this path of light. Any words without actions just lead us back to the beginning of our journey. Each of us as an embodiment of light is here to learn to love ourselves and others. To recognise our truth and have it shine as a beacon to the world. There is no perfect being incarnated. For that to be so would defeat the object of this classroom that we call life. It is recognised that some are further along the path than others. but part of our path is to help fellow travellers along the journey not race ahead and leave them to stumble through life there are no crowns to wear and no being shall perch themselves above others. In the past few days, I have been saddened by those who found themselves a pedestal then perched upon as if to stand above the masses. This is not true knowledge it is just an illusion. Clarity of thought and deed is always our greatest aim.

Blessings.

Mist of Doubt

Oh, Greatest of Lights I am lost. I travel my path which was cast by your very hand. The shadows seem so long and the light so far. I feel your hand rest gently on my shoulder. My heart is filled with your love and light. I have faith when all is lost, I just have faith to take another step. To know deep down that all is love. that you will not let me fall. That with each step and with each breath I take another may find the light within. that their tears of pain turn to tears of joy. that they may find the strength to stand once more to continue their journey. Oh, most Holy I ask not for me but for my friends who fear for an uncertain future, where the mists of doubt surround their view. Give them strength, give them love and peace. Bless them with your love and keep them wrapped within your heart. Thank you.

Amen

. ° ° . ° ° .
° ▪ ▪ ▪ °

This Life

It goes too fast. It was only yesterday I
breathed my first breath. All the tears of joy
and tears of sorrow I have wept for forgotten
faces. Now I see the approaching nightfall
and breathe a sigh of relief. It was my
greatest love and my darkest fear. As death
calls my name, I will shed no tear.

Take just a minute to glance to heavens to
give thanks for all the blessings in your life.
your family your friends. Those that hold
you in their heart. The food on your table
and the shelter you have. To hear the
laughter of children. or the words from a
loved one. All worthy of thanks.

Love is love and spirit is spirit. When man
questions every symbol as positive or
negative we lose something. In life,
something's just are. It's so easy and so
simple to just love, to say thank you or sorry
and even I was wrong yet sometimes we are

so wrapped up in our own world we forget
the most important gestures. A child gazes at
their parents with unconditional love. No
questions, no doubts. Just complete trust. yet
we build walls as we grow. Just love and be
love. it is not that hard.

At some point in your life, the universe will
gently guide to where you are meant to be.
To place you in a position where the whole
of your life has led up to this point. All
learning positive and negative has made you
the person you are today. This enables you
to immerse yourself completely in the
oncoming experience. Fear and nerves are
that of the personality. The inner recognises
and understands the reason for this event.to
the universe time and distance have no
meaning some events where forecast from
the moment of incarnation... and your whole
journey has brought you to this point. so,
now you should walk forward without fear
and have complete trust in the universe.
even though the personality deems it not
rational. For fear is just the unknown. With
love, light and truth it shall be overcome.
Blessings.

The Greatest of Lights gave a priceless gift
to each soul born upon the realm of man. He
named that gift mother. Mothers are
heaven`s angels in disguise. Their only gift
is unconditional love from the first cry of a
newborn soul until their final breath on this
mortal coil.

From the chaos of the universe, I emerged
plunged into this nightmare called life. I
seek only peace and love. yet the world
taunts my every attempt. I walk buried deep
within my own truth. people come and
people go but this life last cannot last
forever and once more I am cast back into
the void of divine consciousness

For I stood upon the earth and gazed into the
heavens and the name of every soul ever
created was written upon the stars.

I found true knowledge locked within my
heart and I shared it with the world

we are responsible for our own choices in
life whether they be right or wrong. Man's

44

ego and pride so often steps in to prevent us from obtaining truth and happiness. yet we often later look back with great sadness and regret for that moment of opportunity has passed. so, we return to the learning cycle once again. To know true wisdom is to look into your heart and choose without bias or annoying traits of the personality what you want for your future before that moment becomes an echo of the past and we end up sitting alone with thoughts of what might have been!!

To be given the gift of love from another is the highest compliment known to mankind. Take care not to discard this with such ease as it surely meant nothing. In truth, love and hate are such strong emotions and there is a very thin line between both. Never get the two confused. To hate is to lose all respect for the existence of that person.to love is give your entire being for another. The path of these emotions is so fraught with perils one wrong step or word and in the end, the only person you are fooling is yourself. So, tread carefully for karma watches you at every turn!

Sometimes our greatest lesson is the one we are too blind to see.

There are three sides to every story. yours, theirs and the truth. it's better to listen to all sides then live in false judgment Ego and emotion can change the way we look at the truth, it casts a shadow over our vision of any real truth.

Oh, Shadows of the World

Have you ever looked at the pain you bring?
Did you hear the song of sorrow the angels
sing? Did you see the tears fall and hearts
broken?
Did you listen to so many prayers spoken?
The blood you spilt in no Gods name. What
was the point what did you gain? Broken
lives and tortured souls. Carnage and
mayhem your only goal
Now angels weep as man cries out Lost in
darkness, so full of doubt your just the
shadows, no light you hold.
Just Full of hate, as you spread the lies your
told
the Gods light still burns the flame of love.
As they Watch over us from above.
As mankind strives once more for peace So
all their pain can find release.

. . . .

I am strange

I know I am strange. I see the world not as
you do. I know all the names you have
called me. Because you kindly carved them
on my heart. you made me walk alone
because I was not like you. Weirdo, Freak,
Fatso, stick boy, Geek. Was that the best
you could do? you gave me all these names
but you never asked me my own. I didn't
dress like you and that wasn't right. I didn't
like the same things as you and that wasn't
right. Too brainy, too dumb, too tall, too
small. Was It so right to shout my
differences to the world? you didn't know
my truth so you just made it up. Then
spreading lies to all who would listen. I
became your version of my truth not that of
my own. Was I so scary you could not even
say hello? Now I wonder what scares you
the most was it me.

Or what your idea of me brought out in you.
I am worth a hundred million of you. I can

now look in a mirror and love the person
staring back. I wonder if you can, or does
your conscience plague you. thank you for
showing me the sort of person I would never
want to be. Because if you are what is called
normal I would rather be the freak that you
so nicely named me. Remember it is the
weirdo's like me that changed the world.

Teacher

I did not come into this world to teach you
the path.
I only came to guide, for as much as you I
seek to understand.
We shall walk this rocky path together.
you shall learn from all the times I have
stumbled.
I shall learn from all the tears you have
wept.
I am no better than you.
Hardly a wise guru hidden from the world.
We are just souls taking a stroll together.
We have both seen such love and light.
Also, such tears and shadows.
Yet we still walk on. We never give up.
When you fall, I will be there to help you
stand.
When I falter at the lord's many tests.
you will be there to give me strength to
carry on once more.
So, we will walk in peace up this mountain
of truth.

one step at a time. Side by side so we can reach the summit together.

In a Time Now Passed

I look across this courtyard made of stone.
Tears fill my eyes as the chains bind my
wrists.
We are so close yet so far.
Banned from this place ,this love and this
time.
I hear the scarlet dragon scream in pain and
anguish overhead.
The banners of a new rule fly upon the
castle walls.
We will not forget, we will return.
No time or space will forbid this.
Our love will cross the oceans and
mountains.
Each life reborn will draw us back to this
blessed place.
To put right all past sins.. to light the candle
of truth once more.

I haven't forgotten. I hear their call.
Lady, I await your presence.

I ask you?

What difference does it make to you who I
love, be it man or woman?
What difference does it make to you where I
pray, Church Temple or Forest Grove what
difference does it make to you the colour of
my skin, black, white or brown? What
difference does it make to you the place I
was born?
Germany, France, Iran. What difference
does it make to you the language I speak?
English, Arabic, Chinese. What difference
does it make to you who I choose to wear?
Suit, dress, burka. What difference does it
make to you the faith I have? One God,
many Gods, no God. What difference does it
make to you how I live my life? In work or
in prayer,
I see you have no answers.
If you have no answers then you have no
right to judge me.

A Thousand Years

I waited a thousand years to find you.

When you stood just before my eyes.

The Heavens rejoiced upon the day we met.

As we unlocked the secrets we had kept.

Now were joined together no man or god
may part.

when I gazed into your eyes I knew I had
lost my heart.

For you , I am ever thankful no greater gift
was shared.

you taught me how to love again, you
showed me how to care.

So, thank you for being me, it is strange, yet
so true.

Just always remember deep within my soul
belongs to you.

Just One

One soul, one love, one heart, born as one to
never part, sent by God his will our task,
drawn by a love from our past. Our eyes met
and our lips touched, felt like I had known
you forever. It was so natural no fuss no
stress, we knew at that moment we were
blessed. I'm you and your me, our hearts
joined in love. For the world to see, a gift
from above for you and me. I close my eyes
and see your face; a single touch fills me
with grace. A love so pure, our hearts so
true, we really are the chosen few.

Never give up on your heart.
Just because it did not work in the past does
not mean it will not work in the future. It's
easy to build walls around yourself through
fear of new heartache, but every being on
earth was given the ability to love another.
It would be a shame not to use it.

Oh Lord

Walking in the shadows, I stumble with each
step. My eyes search for the light of Heaven.
Each sunrise my heart gladdens in the
knowledge that I am one day closer to going
home.
I am so tired of walking this path. Oh, Lord
is it so wrong to want to leave all this
behind. When the only love, you know is
Divine love.
This realm you made is a lonely place.
Yet another day dawns and another step
along my path is taken. I have so much to
give thanks for.
The souls who taught me lessons good and
bad. The love I was shown as travellers
passed me by.
They come and they go this is the way of the
journey we all take.
So, I will walk on once more. To greet the
dawn of a new day. Knowing you walk
beside me.
Never seen but always felt.

Thank you

Did you think I had forgotten you? Did you think I could walk away? Each Night you fill my dreams, your wings enfold me. Covering me in peace, so I am hidden from this world. Some days I am not strong enough for this task I was set. Yet you fill my heart with love and courage. you are my strength, my outstretched hand when the shadows draw near. you are ever present, my shadow of contentment and my place to hide each day. When I feel unworthy of your presence you never leave. always standing filling me with love.

Each day I despair at this path I walk, always feeling alone. Yet deep down I know I am loved and cared for. I am privileged to have many amazing souls walk into my world. My heart rejoices at your song to the heavens. So, for this, I give thanks, for your wondrous being that walk beside me. For those who stole my heart and captured my

soul. Thank you for never giving up on me.
For helping me stand when I could not.

Thank you

Pain

Past pain is something we all carry. It can consume every second of our existence. we fear that if we let go of the pain, we will lose the memory of those things most cherished, this is not so.
Nothing within the bounds of the universe can break those chains of love.
What once was shall always be. For the love and peace of those times dwell within our very soul.
To remember those times of joy is a blessing. the sadness that we wrap these events in taints the beauty of their existence. love has no bounds, it does not heed the realms of time and space. we love and therefore we are loved.

Circles

Sometimes in our lives, we walk in circles.
we do not realise we are doing it.
Time after time we return to the same
pattern. Just repeating the same actions. Fear
or doubt stops us from letting go of that old
comfy firm foundation and heading for
pastures new.
What if I fail?
What if it's the same old grass that is on this
side of the hill?
These are questions we ask ourselves as we
settle deeper into our safe little corner of the
world.
It is easy to dream but to make your dream a
reality is a whole different matter.
In truth, we do not know what the next day
will bring into our lives.
Is it not better to take baby steps towards
that dream which plays out in your head day
after day?

If you never try you will never know. The only thing that ever stops us moving forward is the fear of failure. We never really fail it just a baby step backwards.

Blessings

Lord

Did you ever question the truths you have
been told?
Are those fluffy angels we call upon so
often. Really the hosts of heaven?
Have you ever seen a real angel? Felt its
presence cleanse your soul?
When you stand within its purest light.
humbled by its glory.
Well, what about fairies? Those cute and
harmless beings
mother nature's little helpers.
Without guile and without sin
to seek yet not to question is to not seek at
all.
So, I ask you just to take a minute and
question your belief, not of god or goddess
or man, but the knowledge that you come
upon when travelling this land.
The shadows we cast in this world effect our
closest.
Yet in times of hardship and pain, we call to
the heavens for peaceful release.

The Gods within bring peace to our worlds
yet we still search the sky looking for that
sign of acceptance.
In times of sorrow and pain, we seek just a
helping hand to guide us onto the next step
on our path.
Accept the divinity within for sure they will
cast a blazing light to banish all shadows.
Lord. I have such faith in your council and
your love. Yet each day as I take another
step into the future.
I have fear. We are all confident of our path
in life when we portray ourselves to the
outside world, but as you know we all have
doubts and we all question the choices we
make.
If it is made with the heart then it is
normally correct.
Yet this does not stop the pain of being
alone. or saying goodbye to something we
held so dear.
Then we are alone having to face the reality
of the choice we made.
Our friends and family stand by us and give
us the love we need but in the end, there is
just us. kept from sleep or rest through the
fear of an unknown future.

Oh, greatest of light give me your strength
and love in these times.
Bless all those who have helped me walk
this path.
Thank you, Lord.
Amen

Blessings

With whispered humility, I kneel before ye.
The Birds of Heaven sing their song of
blissful praise. Glory unto thee oh most holy
of lights.
Blessings be upon my fellow travellers and
those who have touched my soul for they
have given me the greatest gift known which
is that of love. watch over them as they
travel on their path. For they honour thy
name and bring forth the greatest of lights.

I felt you so near. yet your face was
shrouded in mist. My heart touched yours.
Our souls sang the song of the wise. The
feelings of remembrance echoed through my
being. I called unto the most high. Oh, lord
please reveal this soul so akin. and then you
were gone. Like waking from a dream. just a
fading memory. until we meet again my
Lady of the mist.
Blessings.

Burden

Sometimes it is not anger you carry it is just
sadness.
The burden you carry is so heavy and you
have walked with it for so long its seems an
eternity.
you look at the lives around you and think
some people have such hardships.
How can I possibly complain in the face of
the pain that some carry?
Yet days when I sit alone and see no end to
this lesson I am taking.
It is so difficult to not raise your voice to the
heavens and say lord is it really meant to be
so hard?
Have I not done enough? To stand alone on
the journey you take is the most frightening
thing.
Many stand by my side as blessed and so
loved friends yet they still do not truly
understand.
How could they? We all walk our own
paths.

Every so often I see this amazing light at the
end of the tunnel and in the blink of an eye,
it is gone.
Maybe this is how my life is meant to run its
course, but I pray to the greatest of lights
that are not.
Namaste.

Questioned

How many times have you questioned your life?
How many times have you sat down at the end of the day and asked yourself what is going on in your life at that present time? I have done these countless times.
When I am truly lost and wander aimlessly. hoping that behind all this apparent confusion there is a divine plan laid out just for me. this has taken more courage and patience than I ever believed.
It is so hard to have faith when you feel truly lost. I have spoken many times to the lord above. but I do sometimes wonder if he is listening or has he left his phone on the answering machine when he knows I am going to call.
This does not make my faith any less, it is right to question everything. I do wonder though can we question god about our own life progression.

My belief is one thing that I have never questioned.
Yes, there are days when everything is going wrong and nothing makes sense where I do want to give up on everything and go hide in the cupboard and lock out the world. But mostly on days when life is so hard I look into my heart and whisper Lord I hope you know what you are doing because I do not have a clue.

Patterns

Sometimes events happen in our lives. these
are times that touch your very soul and leave
you with more questions than answers. That
feeling of déjà vie appears as if to say have I
done this before. The most famous of
sayings ring out to the world. they never
learn. they always do this. for that is the
only measure of truth. As it is written and
this is truth. Am I repeating myself?
These events are not a result of patterns that
you have formed in your life.
To give these occurrences that title is too
easy.
We all have patterns and things we need to
overcome.
But that makes us who we are.
It is so easy for others to judge us on our
patterns.

So, I often think when I see people
following patterns in their life.

Well, what is a pattern and what is a life event? Who can tell the difference for surely not I?
YOU HAVE TO FOLLOW YOUR HEART.

...

If people then rush to judge you remember they only see one side of your story.
Don't we all deserve some form of happiness even if it lasts a small amount of time?
Who are we to say NO that wasn't real it was just you repeating yourself once more?

Judge not less ye be judged yourself.
Blessings

Wait

I stand still. Why I wait I have no reason. I took off my sandals and rested on this place of peace.
I've journeyed long and far. For so many moons my life has changed. This was foreseen and foretold by my very breath.
I look to the heavens for a sign to continue my journey.
Yet, still, I wait.
New souls join me each day full of love and light eager to join the most high.
Yet, still, I wait.
I found a heart so sacred so full of light I was blinded, humbled to the very core to be in such presence. Yet now was not the time.
So, I will wait.
Time and distance have no power over the path of the soul. Pain and anger do not vanish without understanding. the gift of understanding does not come without time.
So, my greatest of lights.
Here, I will wait.

Kneel

I kneel before ye oh greatest of lights and I give thanks unto thee for my friends for my love of life and for each new day that gladdens my heart. Keep safe all the beautiful souls that have crossed my path.

For they are they carry the torch of pure truth that shines amongst the darkest of corners.

Amen

Never Forget

Lord, I pray I never forget the souls who
have crossed my path. For they have given
me so much.
I know as time passes we move forward and
change but give me strength to remember
those who touched my life, for without them
I would not have grown.
So many of us enjoy a life experience then
forget the actions that empowered us.
Please let me give thanks for those people
and times.

Amen.

Better or Worse

Are some experiences so bad we have to
cast them from our mind and pretend they
never happened?
Does this make us change our complete
character?
From a loving being to someone scared of a
life event because of what it brought out in
us.
Are we better for the experience or worse?
May we not forget those who have entered
our lives, those who made us laugh and
those who made us cry.
Let us be thankful for those who brought
such love and light into a dark world. Even
if they have walked on.
Let us always remember their memory and
if they should cross our path once more
rejoice in the love that they bare for we are
never truly alone.

Blessings.

Yours, Theirs, and the Truth

There are three sides to every story. yours,
theirs and the truth.
It is better to listen to all sides then live in
false judgment.
Ego and emotion can change the way we
look at the truth, it casts a shadow over our
vision of any real truth.
Sometimes we all have to take a step back
and remember why we chose to walk this
path of light.
Words without actions just lead us back to
the beginning of our journey.
Each of us as a being is here to learn to love
ourselves and others.
To recognise our truth and have it shine as a
beacon to the world.
There is no perfect being incarnated, for that
to be so would defeat the object of this
classroom called life.

It is recognised that some are further along the path than others, but part of our path is to help fellow travellers along the journey not race ahead and leave them to stumble through life. There are no crowns to wear and no being shall perch themselves above others.

In the past few days, I have been saddened by those who found themselves a pedestal then perched upon as if to stand above the masses.

This is not true knowledge it is just an illusion. Clarity of thought and deed is always our greatest aim.

Blessings

Heavens

OH, GREATEST OF LIGHTS. I was born
to do your will.
Use my eyes to gaze upon the glory of the
heavens and this earth you created.
Use my ears to hear your voice that echoes
upon the winds.
Use my mouth to speak of my love of your
majesty.
Use my hands to help those that have fallen
back onto the path.
Use my back to carry the burden of others so
they may rest for a while.
Use my legs to continue upon this path I
tread.
Use my feet to follow in the footsteps of
those who have gone before me.
Use my soul to blaze a light into the darkest
of corners. Lord, I am thine.

Give me Strength

Lord, I pray I never forget the souls who
have crossed my path.
For they have given me so much.
I know as time passes we move forward and
change but give me the strength to
remember those who touched my life for
without them I would not have grown.
So many of us enjoy a life experience then
forget the actions that empowered us.
Please let me give thanks for those people
and times.

Amen.

Torch

I kneel before ye oh greatest of lights and I
give thanks unto thee for my friends for my
love of life and for each new day that
gladdens my heart.
Keep safe all the beautiful souls that have
crossed my path.
For they are they carry the torch of pure
truth that shines amongst the darkest of
corners.
Amen.

Silence

Close your eyes quieten your mind.
Within the silence you will find.
The loving touch of a tender heart.
This is where our dreams do start.
A place of joy, no fear or pain.
Where love once lost returns again. The
memory carried throughout the years.
Has brought you peace and calmed your
fears.
Know your loved and your souls so near.
That twilight touch to draw you here.

Who am I?

I'm the one who stands alone.
I'm the one for good or bad you cannot
forget I'm the one who holds your hand
when you're sad.
I'm the one who's filled with joy when you
laugh.
I'm the one who loves you all.
I'm the one who touches your soul.
I'm the one who does the gods work.
I'm the one you have met before.
I'm the one who's blessed to have met u
I'm the one who will walk gods path I'm the
one who knows why?
I'm the one who is not worthy of you .
Blessings to you all.

Darkness

I hear your voice in the darkness.
When in times of confusion you seek
guidance.
Just know that I stand by your side.
I am unseen and unheard but ever present
only those rare few upon this realm, may
gaze upon my true being.
Many souls enter your life.
Some bring great tidings of love and light,
while others bring hardship and pain.
Each meeting brings a lesson a chance to
learn about your path in this world.
For good or bad.
In times of great sorrow and loss, it is hard
to not judge others with harshness.
When all else is lost, man looks to
themselves.
their own inner needs and desires. To love
oneself is a hard lesson to learn.
You're a being of light and love conceived
in the glory of the heavenly realm yet you
forget this as earthly burdens weigh heavily
on your shoulders.

The soul cries out at the loss of a loved one.
Then darkness descends into your life.
Have an understanding that I am here.
I will guide you through all your days upon
this path you travel.
I will guard you while you rest.
For I am Love.
For I am light.
Blessings

Right Over Might

It must be always Right Over Might for any other road leads to the shadows. when mankind takes what he desires with force, the pain of the innocent sings out across the world. It takes just one man to save the world, it also takes one man to reduce the world to ashes. I do not understand how you feel you can justify the deeds that are done. When war is waged. Do you not see or feel the suffering of those you have just walked over? Did your conscience leave you when you came into power? War answers nothing. peace must prevail for mankind to evolve.

Your Shadow

Though I walk in your shadow. I feel your soul aflame with the light of the almighty. Through time and space, we travel, the years and lives pass like fleeting moments always close by. Our hearts and souls echo through eternity, as we walk the path of remembrance. Hoping each new life will be our last and we can finally rejoin and be at peace. I wait with baited breath and the joy of the heavens for your return. For blessed are we to have known such light, and to walk the path of the wise.

25024055R00050

Printed in Great Britain
by Amazon